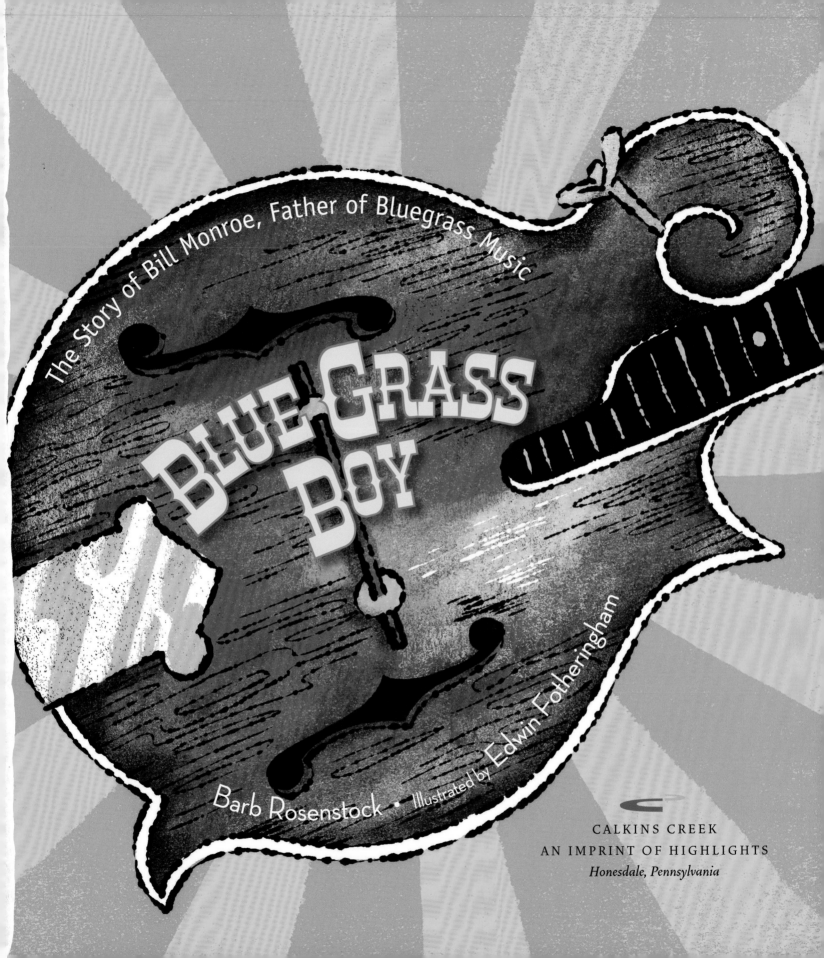

The Story of Bill Monroe, Father of Bluegrass Music

BLUE GRASS BOY

Barb Rosenstock • Illustrated by Edwin Fotheringham

CALKINS CREEK
AN IMPRINT OF HIGHLIGHTS
Honesdale, Pennsylvania

For my brother, a country boy at heart
   —BR

For my family
      —EF

Calkins Creek
An Imprint of Highlights
815 Church Street
Honesdale, Pennsylvania 18431

Printed in China
ISBN: 978-1-62979-439-6
Library of Congress Control Number: 2017940085

First edition
The text of this book is set in ITC Officina Sans.
The illustrations are digital.
10 9 8 7 6 5 4 3 2 1

"THOSE TUNES ARE ALL IN THE AIR.
I JUST HAPPENED TO BE THE FIRST ONE TO PICK THEM OUT."

—Bill Monroe

THE MONROE FAMILY WORKED HARD

in that bluegrass state of Kentucky—plowing and
mining its rolling hills. Willie was the youngest,
following his seven brothers and sisters like a
runt pup squirming to fit in.

It didn't help that his bright blue eyes crossed. His brothers teased, strangers pointed and laughed—thinking since Willie's eyes didn't work right, his ears didn't either.

Truth was, Willie owned the hardest-working
ears in that whole country. When his ears heard
trouble coming—the rustle of sneaky footsteps or
the squeak of an unfamiliar wagon wheel—Willie
hightailed it to the barn and hid for hours . . .

until cheerful jigs, graceful hymns, and lilting ballads soared across the cornfields. A sundown jamboree! Mother fiddled the old tunes on the front porch, toes tapping in time. Uncle Pen shuffled the fiddle too. Daddy buck-danced to the beat and Willie joined the rest, singing harmonies that echoed through the hollows.

The year Willie turned ten, the music stopped.
Mother took sick and died. Willie knew she
wasn't coming back. He heard it in the silence.

In fields and forests, he searched for sounds to heal his heart. Willie tuned his ears to rushing streams, wailing winds, the sharp *tu-wee* of a flycatcher's cry.

He sang the hill sounds, calling loud,
yet so high and gentle that cotton-tailed
rabbits turned, but didn't run.

One brother laid claim to Mother's fiddle;
another bought a beat-up guitar.

Willie found an old mandolin lying around. He learned to strum and tune its strings to E, A, D, and G. Willie closed his eyes and played along with memories of Mother.

His brothers and sisters left for better jobs in bigger cities.
Willie and Daddy stayed behind—whistling trains and barking
foxhounds their only company. When Willie turned sixteen,
Daddy too passed on.

Willie became known as "Bill"—it made him sound grown.

Bill and his mandolin moved up
to Uncle Pen's cabin.

On weekdays he split wood and carried water; on Saturdays the two saddled a mule and rode out to play hillside dances. Wherever Uncle Pen and Bill went, folks shoved back furniture, rolled up carpets, and hollered "Do-si-do!"

Bill met Arnold Shultz—the most famous traveling picker in those parts. Arnold played the blues. His calloused fingers flew up and down a fiddle or a guitar neck like a flock of blackbirds. From Arnold, Bill learned to bend and slide notes—smooth to shivery. His ears took Arnold's rhythms to heart, thumping til the sun came up.

At eighteen, Bill joined his brothers near the booming city of Chicago, washing oil drums in a refinery.

When his brothers started a band, Bill joined in and
spent the next ten years playing other people's music.

But Bill's hard-working ears never stopped collecting.
Chirps. Taps. Whistles. Be-bop. Big band. Blues.
Hundreds, thousands, maybe millions of sounds filled
Bill's head—until one day they overflowed!

Introducing . . .

THE BLUE GRASS BOYS!

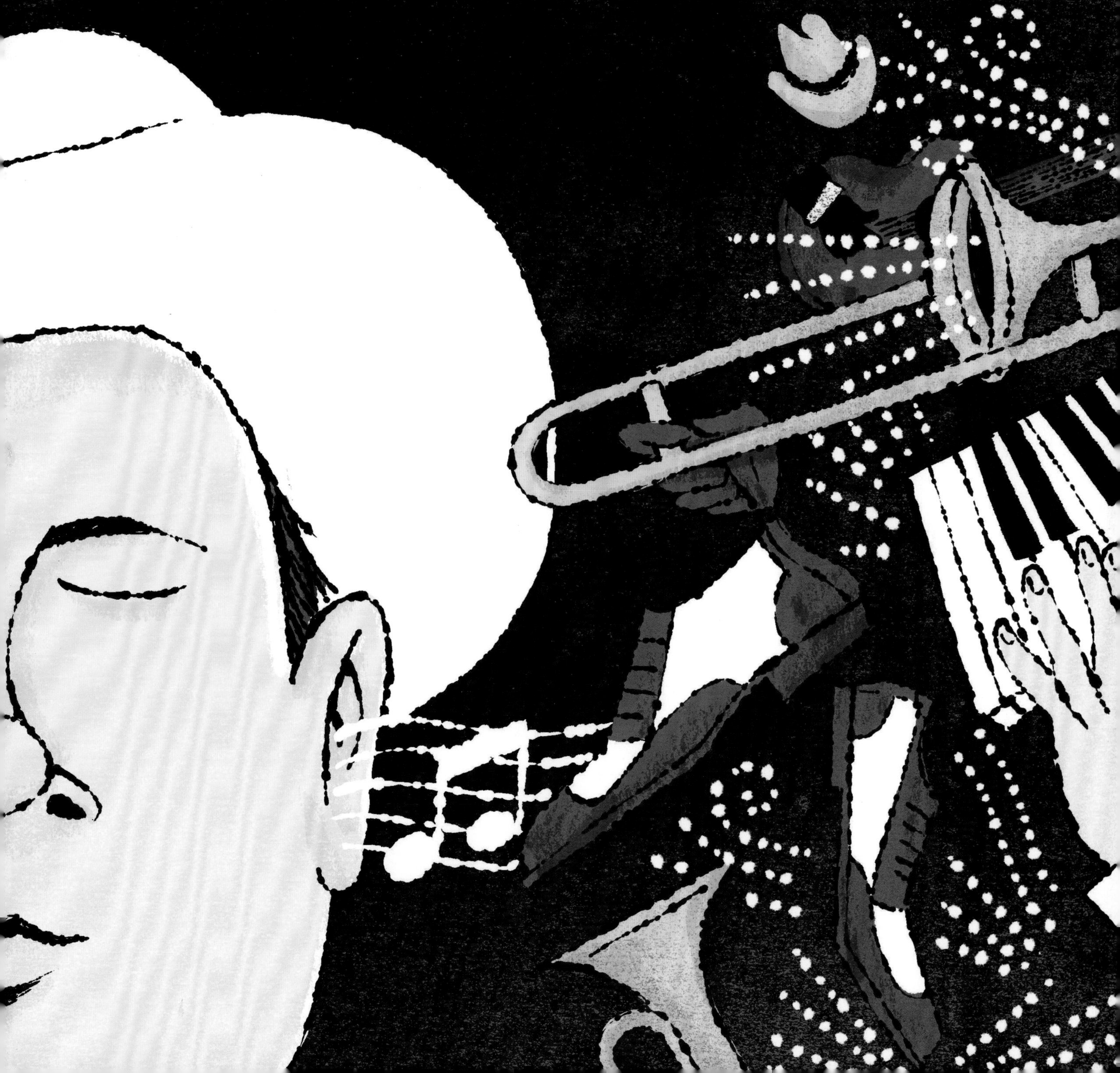

Bill's very own band! A guitarist, a fiddler, and an upright bassist, with Bill playing mandolin.

The Blue Grass Boys cleaned out a gas station's old grease shed, added a few seats, and searched for a new sound.

Started. Stopped.
Started again.
Bill's ears knew the sound
wasn't perfect.

He looked for an instrument
to rush the music along like a
mountain stream—and found it
in the banjo!

Bill took his Blue Grass Boys from that grease shed,
on the road, all the way to the stage of Nashville's
Grand Ole Opry—the greatest country-singing, folk-dancing,
live radio jamboree in the USA!

On the *Opry* stage, Bill chopped the mandolin in perfect time
with his heartbeat. The fiddle shuffled, the guitar strummed,
the bass thumped, and the banjo shot a stream of notes
straight into the audience. Bill sang of love and loneliness,
calling loud over the instruments, yet so high and gentle that
the crowd went wild!

Young folks stepped in the aisles.
Grown folks stomped in their seats.

The music plowed through the radio,
touching city folks missing the hills
and hill folks left in the hollows. A sound
entirely new, yet familiar as a front porch.

That night, and for thousands of nights after,
audiences all over the world cheered for Bill Monroe,
whistling and hollering for his new music—

the sweet sound of bluegrass.

"I WAS JUST GONNA CARVE OUT A MUSIC OF MY OWN, DIFFERENT FROM ANYBODY ELSE'S MUSIC. I DIDN'T WANNA COPY ANYBODY . . ."
—Bill Monroe

Monroe's mother, Malissa Vandiver Monroe (seated), with two of her grandchildren and Bill and his sister Bertha, about 1920.

William Smith "Bill" Monroe was born to James Buchanan "Buck" and Malissa Vandiver Monroe on September 13, 1911. There were seven older children: Harry, Speed, John, Maude, Birch, Charlie, and Bertha. The Monroe family grew corn and tobacco while also operating a portable sawmill and small coal mine on over six hundred acres of land in western Kentucky, near the town of Rosine.

Bill was born with a left eye that turned inward (*esotropia*), resulting in poor depth perception and blurriness. Doctors at the time thought children would grow out of this condition, but Bill did not. Monroe's superb hearing likely resulted from his struggle to see.

When Bill was ten, his mother died, probably from a spinal disease. Within a year or two, he'd stopped attending school and drove lumber wagons for relatives and neighbors.

His earliest musical influences were his mother and her brother, "Uncle Pen" (James Pendleton Vandiver, 1869–1932), a well-known dance fiddler in the area. Monroe was also strongly influenced by Arnold Shultz (1886–1931), an African-American blues guitarist and fiddler.

In 1930, Monroe left the hills to work at the Sinclair refinery in northern Indiana, near Chicago. He had surgery to fix his eye, but needed thick glasses and did not learn to read music, so all his arrangements were created by ear. He joined brothers Birch and Charlie, playing as "The Monroe Brothers" at parties and square dances on tours arranged by local radio stations. In 1934, while Birch stayed at the refinery, Charlie and Bill left their factory jobs to play music full time on the radio, in concerts, and recording for the Bluebird label, a subsidiary of RCA Victor.

The Monroe Brothers broke up in 1938 over personal and artistic differences. Bill went in search of his own musical style—a sped-up combination of Scots-Irish fiddle tunes, country string band music, gospel, blues, and jazz. In 1939, Bill Monroe and his Blue Grass Boys won a spot on Nashville's *Grand Ole Opry*. Though the musicians in the band changed frequently, the 1945–48 combination solidified this new musical genre (Bill Monroe on mandolin, Earl Scruggs on banjo, Chubby Wise on fiddle, Lester Flatt on guitar, and Howard Watts on bass).

Pendleton "Uncle Pen" Vandiver (left) with Clarence Remus Wilson. Wilson's daughter Flossie Wilson Hines (center) and friends stand behind.

Arnold Shultz (left) and Clarence Remus Wilson.

These and other musicians eventually went out on their own, playing in a similar style. By the mid-1950s, it came to be known as "bluegrass music." Monroe's pioneering chord structures, unique runs, and syncopated rhythms influenced the future of popular music. The high, close harmonies, instrumental solos, and driving beat of bluegrass changed country music and led to the development of rock and roll. The flip side of Elvis Presley's first single, "That's All Right," was his version of Monroe's song "Blue Moon of Kentucky." Other famous musicians influenced by Monroe include Johnny Cash, Buddy Holly, Carl Perkins, Chuck Berry, The Everly Brothers, and Jerry Garcia.

Bill Monroe is the only musician inducted into the Country Music Hall of Fame, the Rock and Roll Hall of Fame, the International Bluegrass Museum's Hall of Fame, *and* the Nashville Songwriters Hall of Fame. He received the Grammy Lifetime Achievement Award in 1993 and the National Medal of the Arts in 1995. He appeared on the *Opry* stage for fifty-six years, retiring only after suffering a series of strokes that led to his death on September 9, 1996. He's buried with his mother, father, all seven siblings, and Uncle Pen in the Rosine Cemetery in western Kentucky.

You can hear bluegrass music every day on TV, in movies, or in video games. Thousands of musicians gather in hundreds of towns in the US and across the world to sing and pick at bluegrass festivals. But if you ever get a chance to wander through western Kentucky, close your eyes and tune your ears to the wind, the streams, and the birds. The hills sound like bluegrass, the music of Bill Monroe.

Bill Monroe and the Blue Grass Boys around 1946–47.

"IT'S SCOTCH BAGPIPES AND OLE-TIME FIDDLIN'.
IT'S METHODIST AND HOLINESS AND BAPTIST. IT'S BLUES AND JAZZ, AND IT
HAS A HIGH LONESOME SOUND. IT'S PLAIN MUSIC THAT TELLS A GOOD STORY.
IT'S PLAYED FROM MY HEART TO YOUR HEART, AND IT WILL TOUCH YOU."
—Bill Monroe

BIBLIOGRAPHY

Bartenstein, Fred, Gary Reid, et al. *The Bluegrass Hall of Fame: Inductee Biographies 1991–2014*. Louisville, KY: Holland Brown, 2014.

Black, Bob. *Come Hither to Go Yonder: Playing Bluegrass with Bill Monroe*. Urbana: University of Illinois Press, 2005.

Bragg, Rick. "A Balladeer of Bluegrass Is Now Gone Yet Lives On." *New York Times*, November 4, 1996. nytimes.com/1996/11/04/us/a-balladeer-of-bluegrass-is-now-gone-yet-lives-on.html.

Cantwell, Robert. *Bluegrass Breakdown: The Making of the Old Southern Sound*. Urbana: University of Illinois Press, 1984.

Country Music Hall of Fame® and Museum. "Bill Monroe." Adapted from *Encyclopedia of Country Music*, ed. Michael McCall, John Rumble, and Paul Kingsbury. Oxford: Oxford University Press, 2012. Accessed February 18, 2014. countrymusichalloffame.org/Inductees/InducteeDetail/bill-monroe.

Dawidoff, Nicholas. *In the Country of Country: A Journey to the Roots of American Music*. New York: Vintage Books/Random House, 1998.

Erbsen, Wayne. *Rural Roots of Bluegrass Songs, Stories & History*. Asheville, NC: Native Ground Music, 2003.

Ewing, Tom, ed. *The Bill Monroe Reader*. Urbana: University of Illinois Press, 2000.

Gebhardt, Steve, dir. *Bill Monroe: The Father of Bluegrass*. Winstar, 1999.

Jerusalem Ridge Festival. "The Jerusalem Ridge Festival." Accessed January 10, 2014. jerusalemridgefestival.org/about_jerusalem_ridge.

Klein, Bradley, and Stephanie Coleman. "Bill Monroe: Celebrating the Father of Bluegrass at 100." NPR Music, September 11, 2011. npr.org/2011/09/12/140366232/bill-monroe-celebrating-the-father-of-bluegrass-at-100.

Liebling, Rachel, et al. *High Lonesome: The Story of Bluegrass Music*. United States: Northside Films, 1997.

Lynch, Kevin. "Bluegrass Inventor Bill Monroe (Sept. 13, 1911–Sept. 9, 1996) Springs a Surprise." *No Depression*, September 13, 2013. nodepression.com/article/bluegrass-inventor-bill-monroe-sept-13-1911-sept-9-1996-springs-surprise.

Malone, Bill C., and Judith McCulloh, eds. *Stars of Country Music: Uncle Dave Macon to Johnny Rodriguez*. Urbana: University of Illinois Press, 1975.

Nash, Alanna. *Behind Closed Doors: Talking with the Legends of Country Music*. New York: Alfred A. Knopf, 1988, pp. 327-54.

Ohio County Tourism Commission. "Bluegrass: Bill Monroe Homeplace." Accessed January 10, 2014. visitohiocountyky.com/bill-monroe-homeplace.

Price, Steven D. *Old As the Hills: The Story of Bluegrass Music*. New York: Viking, 1975.

Rock & Roll Hall of Fame. "Bill Monroe." Accessed January 14, 2014. rockhall.com/inductees/bill-monroe.

Rosenberg, Neil V. *Bluegrass: A History*. Urbana: University of Illinois Press, 2005.

Rosenberg, Neil V., and Charles K. Wolfe. *The Music of Bill Monroe*. Urbana: University of Illinois Press, 2007.

Schweizer, Micah. "Bill Monroe's Blue Grass Boys Converge in Kentucky." NPR Music, September 9, 2010. npr.org/templates/story/story.php?storyId=129752861.

Smith, Richard D. *Can't You Hear Me Callin': The Life of Bill Monroe, Father of Bluegrass*. Cambridge, MA: Da Capo Press, 2001.

Smithsonian Folkways. "Bill Monroe: Bluegrass Innovator." Accessed February 13, 2014. folkways.si.edu/explore_folkways/bill_monroe.aspx.

Southern Missouri Bluegrass. "Rosine, KY: Home of Bill Monroe." Accessed February 13, 2014. southernmobluegrass.homestead.com/rosine.html.

Stambler, Irwin, and Grelun Landon. *Country Music: The Encyclopedia*. New York: St. Martin's Press, 1997.

Willis, Barry R. *America's Music, Bluegrass*. Franktown, CO: Pine Valley Music, 1992.

Wolfe, Charles K. *Kentucky Country: Folk and Country Music of Kentucky*. Lexington: University Press of Kentucky, 1996.

ACKNOWLEDGMENTS

Thank you to Fred Bartenstein, bluegrass historian, for his thoughtful reading of the manuscript; Teresa Westfall, Curator of the International Bluegrass Museum, for her comments and research regarding text and art; Keith Baumann of the Old Town School of Folk Music for his gorgeous mandolin playing; and Doug Swartz for his collection of bluegrass and old time recordings. Thankfully, the towns of Bean Blossom, Indiana; Owensboro, Kentucky; and Rosine, Kentucky, have preserved the history of Bill Monroe's life and the ongoing story of bluegrass music. It took a village of bluegrass experts to source and credit the back matter for this book. Special thanks to: Neil V. Rosenberg, Ph.D., Professor Emeritus, Memorial University of Newfoundland; Linda Shaw, Managing Editor, *Bluegrass Unlimited* Magazine; Alan Boehm, Rachel Morris, and Aaron Smithers at Middle Tennessee State; Nancy Cardwell, Roby Cogswell, Cheryl Goatee, Hilda Kossick, and Linda Waterhouse Cook.

SOURCE NOTES

"Those tunes are all in . . ." Smith, p. 389.
"I was just gonna carve . . ." Nash, p. 333.
"It's Scotch bagpipes . . ." Stambler, p. 316.

RESEARCH NOTE

Bill Monroe was a larger-than-life musician, but a very private man. There are as many legends about his childhood and musical beginnings as there are facts. This book uses information from a number of sources written by well-known bluegrass historians. Experts on Monroe's life and music helped me sort through conflicting information.

PICTURE AND TEXT CREDITS

UNCLE PEN

Oh, the people would come from far away
They'd dance all night till the break of day
When the caller hollered "do-si-do"
You knew Uncle Pen was ready to go

Chorus:
Late in the evening about sundown
High on the hill and above the town
Uncle Pen played the fiddle, Lord how it would ring
You could hear it talk, you could hear it sing

He played an old piece he called "Soldier's Joy"
And the one called "The Boston Boy"
The greatest of all was "Jenny Lynn"
To me that's where the fiddle begins

I'll never forget that mournful day
When Uncle Pen was called away
They hung up his fiddle, they hung up his bow
They knew it was time for him to go